Baby Animals

★ A very first picture book ★

The original publishers would like to thank Chilli Bernstein, Milo Clare, and Chanelle Robinson for modeling for this book. Many thanks also to Pampered Pets, Holloway Road, London.

For a free color catalog describing Gareth Stevens Publishing's list of high-quality books and multimedia programs, call 1-800-542-2595 (USA) or 1-800-461-9120 (Canada). Gareth Stevens Publishing's Fax: (414) 225-0377.

Library of Congress Cataloging-in-Publication Data

Tuxworth, Nicola.
    Baby animals: a very first picture book / Nicola Tuxworth.
       p. cm. — (Pictures and words)
    Includes bibliographical references and index.
    Summary: Simple text and photographs present various
baby animals, including a chick, piglet, and kitten.
    ISBN 0-8368-2379-6 (lib. bdg.)
    [1. Animals—Infancy—Juvenile literature. [1. Domestic
animals—Infancy.] I. Title. II. Series.
    QL763.T88   1999
    591.3'9—dc21   98-48808

This North American edition first published in 1999 by
Gareth Stevens Publishing
1555 North RiverCenter Drive, Suite 201
Milwaukee, WI 53212 USA

Original edition © 1997 by Anness Publishing Limited. First published in 1997 by Lorenz Books, an imprint of Anness Publishing Inc., New York, New York. This U.S. edition © 1999 by Gareth Stevens, Inc. Additional end matter © 1999 by Gareth Stevens, Inc.

Managing editor: Sue Grabham
Editor: Roz Fishel
Special photography: Lucy Tizard
Stylist: Marion Elliot
Design and typesetting: Michael Leaman Design Partnership

Picture credits: Warren Photographic/Jane Burton: p. 5, p. 12, p. 13, p. 14, p. 15; Zefa: p. 4 (top), p. 8, p. 9, p. 18, p. 19.

Printed in Mexico

1 2 3 4 5 6 7 8 9 03 02 01 00 99

Baby Animals

★ A very first picture book ★

Nicola Tuxworth

Gareth Stevens Publishing
MILWAUKEE

Chicks

Let me out. I'm hatching.

I'm a baby chicken.

4

Hello, Mom!

Bunnies

I'm a
baby rabbit.
I love crisp
lettuce...

...and
crunchy
carrots.

Time for
a wash...

... and
a great
big hug.

7

Piglets

I'm a baby pig.

My nose is called a snout.

Did someone say "dinner?"

Mmm, it smells good!

Kittens

I'm a baby cat.

Hold still!

Whoops! Have I made a mess?

11

Foals

I'm a
baby
horse.

Look at
my long,
thin legs!

12

Let's play, Mom!

Ducklings

How do you do?

We're baby ducks.

Let's go
for a
swim.

Can I
come,
too?

15

Puppies

I'm a baby dog.

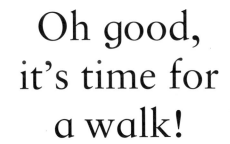

Oh good, it's time for a walk!

16

I'm tired now...

... let's take a
little nap with
teddy bear.

Kids

We're baby goats.

Where
has our
friend
gone?

Here
I am!

19

We're all baby animals. Do you know our names?

bunny

chick

puppy

kitten

duckling

21

Would anyone like to
play with me?

Questions for Discussion

1. Can you think of names for the babies of different kinds of animals, such as sheep, foxes, and bears?

2. How are the baby animals in this book like their mothers? How are they different?

3. Which baby animal in this book is your favorite? Why do you like it best?

4. How do mother animals, like the ones shown in this book, take care of their babies?

5. Which baby animals in this book are mammals that, when they are young, need to drink milk from their mothers? Which baby animals are birds that hatch from eggs? What do these bab   ds eat?

More L oks to Read

The Adventures of Buster the Puppy (series). ako Madokoro (Gareth Stevens)

Amazing Animal Babies. Christopher Maynard (Knopf)

Animals Are Not Like Us (series). Graham Meadows (Gareth Stevens)

Baby Animals. Angela Royston (Aladdin Books)

Cubs and Colts and Calves and Kittens. Allan Fowler (Childrens Press)

Farm Babies. Ann Rice (Grosset & Dunlap)

Real Baby Animals (series). Gisela Buck and Siegfried Buck (Gareth Stevens)

Videos

Animal Babies.
(DK Vision)

Baby Animals.
(Hollywood Select Video)

Baby Animals.
(Vermont Story Works)

Baby Animals Just Want to Have Fun. (Karl-Lorimar)

Web Sites

www.avma.org/care4pets

www.davisfarmland.com/

www.catslife.com/bleustone/
kittendev.html

Some web sites stay current longer than others. For further web sites, use your search engines to locate the following topics: *baby animals, bunnies, chicks, ducklings, foals, kittens, piglets,* and *puppies.*

Glossary-Index

crunchy: having a cracking or crushing sound. (p. 6)

duckling: a baby or young duck. (pp. 14-15, 21)

foal: a baby or young horse, donkey, or zebra. (pp. 12-13)

hatching: coming into life out of an egg. Ducklings hatch from eggs. (p. 4)

kid: a baby or young goat. (pp. 18-19)

mess: something that is dirty or untidy. (p. 11)

piglet: a baby or young pig. (pp. 8-9)

snout: the long front part of an animal's head that points outward and ends with the nose. (p. 8)

24

DOGS

MUTTS

STUART A. KALLEN

ABDO & Daughters

Published by Abdo & Daughters, 4940 Viking Drive, Suite 622, Edina, Minnesota 55435.

Library bound edition distributed by Rockbottom Books, Pentagon Tower, P.O. Box 36036, Minneapolis, Minnesota 55435.

Printed in the United States.

Cover Photo credit: Peter Arnold, Inc.
Interior Photo credits: Peter Arnold, Inc.

Edited by Rosemary Wallner

Library of Congress Cataloging-in-Publication Data

Kallen, Stuart A., 1955
     Mutt / Stuart A. Kallen.
    p. cm. — (Dogs)
Includes bibliographical references (p.24) and index.
  ISBN 1-56239-450-9
1. Dogs—Juvenile literature. [1. Dogs.] I. Title. II. Series: Kallen, Stuart A., 1955-
Dogs.
SF426.5.K35   1995
636.7—dc20   95-928
                                      CIP
                                      AC

ABOUT THE AUTHOR

Stuart Kallen has written over 80 children's books, including many environmental science books.